MW01230273

TOM,
MY SPECIAL GIFT
FROM GOD

ANITA HARGREAVES

ISBN 979-8-89130-062-0 (hardcover)
ISBN 979-8-89130-063-7 (digital)

Christian Faith Publishing
832 Park Avenue
Meadville, PA 16335
www.christianfaithpublishing.com

Printed in the United States of America

My son died in an automobile accident on September 28, 1991. Several people who have heard my story have asked me to write it on paper so others can read it and hopefully benefit from it. I do not consider myself special in any way, just a relatively normal person who has had some very special experiences involving those who have gone before us. My experiences have been similar to those who have described near-death experiences, except that I was never near death while seeing my loved ones.

As a very young girl, I remember sitting by my parents' old Fada radio with my hands folded in prayer and listening to church music. I understood nothing of electronics and imagined there were little people inside that radio making that beautiful music. We moved, and the radio was replaced by a newer one. End of the special music.

Years later, my mother would go to seances conducted by a lady several towns away. Her name was Minnie. I was not allowed to go with Mom, but the seeds of believing in supernatural things were planted. Believing in the spirits of dead people seemed quite natural for me. My mother told me they sang songs and then Minnie would go into a trance and answer questions that had been given to her by those present. In retrospect, I believe my mother went to those seances because her marriage was in trouble.

My mother had been taught to read playing cards by Gypsies she met as a teenage girl. Fortune-telling with cards became a favorite time in our house. My mother died before she could pass her knowledge on to me.

When I was eighteen, I was madly in love with a handsome young man.

We only dated a few times, but he was so special to me. Call it my first love. His father died during the brief time we dated. My girlfriend and I decided to go to the wake. I had never met this young man's parents and had no idea what to expect. There was an open casket.

At the time, I had set up an altar in my bedroom complete with candles and a Bible. I prayed for the young man and his mother and father. The young man I was in love with was already telling me he could not get serious with me because he had college in front of him. I was okay with the college part, but I still wanted to see him. After all, I wanted to go to college also. One of the nights after the funeral, his deceased father appeared to me in a dream. He told me he would "help me" with his son. Well, the help came too late. By the time the young man reentered my life, I was engaged to someone else. So much for young love.

Fast-forward several years… I was married and had two children. My daughter was beautiful and healthy. My son had crossed eyes. By the time he was two, he had had four eye surgeries. I sat by his bed one night and cried. My handsome blue-eyed son with naturally curly blond hair still had crossed eyes. I cried for all the surgeries he had endured, and his eyes still weren't fused. The doctor said he was "cosmetically correct" but that his eyes would cross again when he was tired. He would never fly a commercial airplane. Not the world's biggest problem. There were lots of other things he could do. He had a successful career in engineering and management. But I digress.

A few nights after my crying, I once again had a dream. This time, it was a man's voice that told me, "I will give you the perfect child, but you will only have him a little while." How those words were to haunt me over the years. Was this God speaking to me? Was it Jesus? I can't say. The tone of the voice is not what I remembered. More on that later. It was the words.

True to his words, on January 31, 1969, I gave birth to my third child, a son. We named him Tom. He was a joy from day one. He was loving, so easy to raise, and smart. He didn't do everything perfectly. The words "perfect child" didn't mean perfect as in Jesus but perfect given that he was a child. In thinking back, his brother's and sister's antics had probably desensitized me, and the things Tom did probably didn't bother me. Children can do some not-so-good things at times.

I don't want anyone to think that I didn't or don't love my two other children. I do love them very much. Both have turned into loving adults, each with their own strengths. I would be lost without their love. However, as anyone who has lost a child can tell you, each child is an individual and cannot replace the one who died.

Just a few things about Tom: He was difficult to toilet train. At three, he was still pooping in his diapers. One day, I asked him why he still made messes in his diapers. He told me that his grandma said he was a baby, and he knew babies pooped in their diapers. We had a little talk. I told him that I wanted him to be my big boy, and big boys do not mess up their pants. I told him that if I wanted another baby, I would have one. But I really wanted him to be my big boy. Two days later, he was fully trained.

When he was in first grade, his teacher came to me concerned that Tom wasn't like the other children. When his work assignment was completed, he would sit at his desk, hands folded. The other children would get out of their seats, walk around the room, get books, or play with things in the room. I told her Tom often played "school" with his older sister, and he was waiting for someone (like maybe his teacher) to teach him more.

She got the message and taught him first-, second-, and some third-grade arithmetic by the time the first grade was finished. He then skipped second grade and went right to third grade. That school only went up to the sixth grade, so when the time came, he was bussed to the junior high school in town for math classes.

We lived in Ridgefield, Connecticut, during those years. He competed in a countywide math league and won. When he graduated from Rensselaer Polytechnic Institute as a math major, he landed a job with an actuarial company, which company benefits. He was studying for his fifth actuarial exam when he died.

He was a serious young man. He wasn't what I would call street-smart, but he had wisdom beyond his years. Other parents were pleased when their sons would be with Tom because he was so sensible. Well, he had some failings too.

We had given Tom a car named Nellie. Nellie was a big fat Oldsmobile station wagon. Late one evening, I got a call from the Ridgefield Police. The car was registered in my name. It was found by the garbage dump, and the young man standing by the car was not Tom. The police thought the car was stolen. I assured the police the car was not stolen, but should they happen across my son, to please tell him to return home immediately. Apparently, there had been another car there, but it had beer in it. They had to get rid of the beer before they returned to Nellie.

Tom was a big Mets fan. He played baseball in Little League and loved the game. He was also an Eagle Scout and a member of the National Honor Society. He played football for a while, but his orthopedic doctor said he had a winged scapula and football would not be a good sport for him.

The accident occurred at 3:07 a.m. Tom had driven to Connecticut from New Jersey, where he lived and worked to attend a gathering in honor of a friend who was getting married the next morning. We know he returned home to change his clothes, but from the autopsy we gathered, he did not take time to eat supper. He and the groom and the groomsmen celebrated at a local hamburger restaurant, and yes, he drank more beers than he should have. Around midnight, the group went to a hotel in the next town to visit with people connected with the wedding. I don't recall who. From there, two cars returned to Ridgefield and dropped off one young man at his home.

Interestingly, this was the same young man at the garbage dump with Nellie, the car. Tom and his buddy Erik were in one car, and another friend was in the second car. Both were returning to homes in the same development to sleep. The other car was ahead of Tom's car.

From here things got a little hazy, but Tom swerved for some reason and hit one of the biggest and fattest trees in town. The car hit the tree broadside, not head-on. Tom was killed instantly and so was his best friend.

Erik's father called my phone around 4:20 a.m. It was like my world had stopped. I had been living with a terrible foreboding for about two weeks. I knew something bad was going to happen, and the words in my dream over twenty-two years earlier were on my mind.

Erik was a delightful young man. He was full of joy and spread that joy to others. My family and I welcomed him into our house often. We vacationed with his family. Tom, Erik, their older brothers, and their fathers went on fishing trips to Canada. They talked about car breakdowns, eating mystery meat in Canada, and snakes in the trees. My husband and I had a special place in our hearts for Erik, and his death hurt us deeply. Were they meant to die together? I don't know. How often I thought, *If only Tom had not had his seat belt on, he would have been pushed to Erik's side of the car. The steel door beam would not have punctured Tom's heart and maybe Tom would have prevented Erik from pitching forward to the windshield and doorframe.* Erik was not wearing his seat belt. The if onlys carry so much pain.

I would also like to add that Erik's parents were totally gracious to us, allowing us to use their home as a base to receive our friends. As much as they were hurting, their hearts and home were open to us. One does not forget the love and strength they showed my husband and me.

My husband, Ron, and I are Protestants. Erik had a Catholic funeral. His priest invited us to the front of the church for Communion. We mouthed the words, "We are not Catholic," but the priest insisted we come forward. As I have gotten older, I realize we all worship the same god. That is the important thing. What that priest did in asking us to take Communion has remained with me through the years.

It took me five years of Bible study to come to terms with what happened. I would cry and cry. Then no more tears, and I would think that I had the situation under control. Then the tear ducts would fill up again, and I would cry some more. I have never known such devastation. If you have lost a child, you know what I mean. Children are not supposed to die first. I think of all the parents who have lost children due to accidents, wars, illness, or drugs. I know their pain. One neighbor told me he was very sorry my son died, but he said after six months no one was going to want to hear about it anymore. He hurt me very deeply, but in a way, I understood. One of my cousins lost her son too. She became an alcoholic and died. I decided to write in a journal.

While we were still at the hotel in Connecticut (we were living in Tampa and had to go to Connecticut for the funeral), I had a dream that I heard the telephone ring. I was told to call a certain number to talk with Tom. I couldn't get the numbers straight and never did call them. It was all too raw, and I was a bundle of nerves.

After we returned from the funeral, I was wiped out and stressed beyond belief. On October 6, 1991, I went to bed totally exhausted. Somewhere between 5:00 a.m. and 6:00 a.m., I was awakened by the phone ringing by my bed. At least I thought it was my phone. When I picked up the telephone, all I heard was a dial tone. Because of the botched phone call at the hotel, I knew immediately it had to be Tom trying to reach me.

At any rate, I was now awake and prayed that I would hear from Tom. Here is the part that is the beginning of my communications with Tom. I felt an electrical tingle come over my body like a blanket. Something was pulled out of my chest, yet I was fully aware that I was awake lying on my bed. I found myself in what I would call a spaceship. Not the kind of spaceship our astronauts use to go into space. This was very primitive with wooden benches. There was a pregnant woman who seemed to be like a stewardess. Her face was in the shadows. I have no idea who she was. Although

I never saw him, there was a pilot. We flew into a mist. Again, I heard a telephone ring. This time, someone said it was a telephone call for me. I walked toward the phone. Next to the phone was a large opening like a window without glass. Although I don't recall going through the opening, I believe I did.

The next thing I knew I was in what appeared to me as a large mansion. It reminded me of the Bible verse, "In my Father's house, there are many mansions." The walls and floors were all gray stone. There must have been windows because the room I was in had light. I could see things easily. Tom was standing before me. There was what I would call an older stocky man walking around. He reminded me of a butler type of person I had seen in movies. He said nothing but seemed to be checking that everything was okay.

Tom seemed younger and shorter, and so it was easy for me to put my arms around him. (Interestingly, the autopsy report that arrived at a later date listed Tom at five feet eleven while when alive, he was six feet two). I hugged him and asked if he was happy. His response was "Yes. This is a beautiful place." I asked him what he liked best, and he said, "Months are seven hundred days long." I thought that was weird, but then he had been a math major in college.

The whole time I was with Tom, that electrical tingle was over my body. I knew I was awake, and somehow I knew if I opened my eyes, the visit would end. I kept my eyes closed.

That scene ended, and I found myself in another much larger room. There were rows and rows of what looked like cots or stretchers. There were lots of people on the cots. All were covered with green sheets, including their heads. I went directly to Tom's cot. I knew it was him because there was a lock of blond hair sticking out from the green sheet. I pulled the sheet back, and there he was as in his adult life. I kissed him many times. He did not awaken, but he was breathing! I thought eternal life!

There was a man walking around the room. I felt he was guarding those sleeping. I could tell he did not want me disturbing my son. I then walked to another row of covered sleeping people. I decided to uncover another person. I thought if I saw Tom in the other row, it would be my mind playing tricks on me. As I uncovered the other person, I saw that it was a totally different person. I was relieved.

The next thing I knew, the tingling left me. I knew my visit with my son was over. I opened my eyes. As much as I missed him then, and still miss him, I was happy knowing he was happy and alive in another world.

As an aside, there was a medium in Tampa named Roberta. She told me that my crying kept Tom earthbound. As such, Tom could not do his heavenly work. My mother-in-law told me the story of her mother. She had lost a son as a result of a railroad accident. She had several other children and would care for them as a mother would. After dinner, she would retire to her bedroom and cry. She always wore black. One night as she was ascending the stairs to her room, her son Floyd appeared to her, standing at the top of the stairs. He was carrying two buckets overflowing with what appeared to be water. He said to her, "Mother, these are your tears I have been carrying for you." The next morning, she appeared for breakfast in a brightly colored housedress. The end of tears.

October 19, 1991: While dreaming, I saw Tom at a banquet talking to some people. He was holding a very orange-colored drink. We didn't talk.

It was apparent that I was there as an observer. I thought, *What? No beer?*

Someone gave me a quote from the prophet Khalil Gibran. It said in part, "When you are sorrowful, look again in your heart, and you shall see that in truth you arc wccping for that which has been your delight." How true. I still weep for the wonderful person God gave me. If only he had not taken him from me. My only solace is that he did not suffer when he died.

My daughter called me in early November to say she saw Tom in a dream. She was very excited to see him. She wanted to ask lots of questions, but all he told her was that he wanted to know how she was.

During the Christmas holiday season, my husband and I were driving to Pennsylvania to see our two other children. My husband never met a truck he liked. He felt the need to pass any truck in front of him. Apparently, that is called weaving. He got at least one ticket for it. He never liked my driving, and I did not like the way he drove. Par for the course. I felt myself praying that we would not have an accident. As I was sitting in the passenger seat, I felt the electrical tingle over my body. I knew it was Tom and he was with me. We would arrive safely at our destination.

Shortly before what would have been his twenty-third birthday, I watched a TV show about angels. The lady on the show said God sends us children who are really angels. When they have made a difference in our lives, he takes them back. Is this true? I have no confirmation to prove this either way. It does seem, though, that so many young people who were really great children die early. Naturally, I believe my son was special. Over three hundred people came to his wake and funeral. He didn't seem to have an enemy in the world. Are there other children out there as wonderful as my son? Yes!

I felt Tom's electrical tingle about the same time I was reading a book about angels. That night, around 1:00 a.m., I felt his tinglc. This time I also felt the pressure of his body by my side. Was this because I was reading a book and my mind was playing tricks on me, or was this because my mind was attuned to angels, and it allowed spiritual energies to come to me? I believe it was Tom. Someone else may not.

Back in October, my husband and I picked out a niche for Tom's ashes. We noticed a beautiful eagle flying overhead. We decided to think it was Tom's spirit. Months later, I was watching a TV show. The woman being interviewed said angels can take the form of animals. We decided to believe that the eagle we had seen was Tom's spirit. Was it true? I can't prove it either way, but I will ask Tom when we meet again.

I was doing a lot of reading about angels and the beautiful music in heaven. One night, I was awakened by something gently touching my right cheek. It was so gentle and soft that it did not scare me. I felt immediately that it was an angel. I knew it wasn't my husband, and there wasn't anyone else in the house. The windows were closed, so there was no outside breeze. Suddenly, I heard the most incredibly beautiful violin music. I had never heard that melody before. The music did not last long. Then I heard scales being played. I thanked the angels for proving the book correct.

As time went on, I think I was slowly adjusting to Tom's death, although not knowing what really happened to cause the accident was like having a wound that wouldn't heal. One of the stages of grief is to pass the blame to others. Blaming others helped ease the pain. Something or someone caused Tom's car to hit that tree. I found it easy to blame someone, and that wasn't fair. It was 3:00 a.m.; maybe there was another car involved and maybe not. Tom's car was turbocharged. Did it have a spurt of energy he couldn't control? I think he only had 2,800 miles in the car. Maybe he lost control. Maybe an animal crossed in front of the car, and he swerved? I do not have an answer.

In December of 1992, I had a dream about Tom. I had a phone call from him. All he said was, "It wasn't my fault." I knew immediately he was talking about the accident. Just because he said it wasn't his fault doesn't mean another person was at fault.

Two other things happened during the Christmas holidays. I had misplaced a locket. I had looked high and low for it and finally decided to write about it in my journal. I thought maybe if Tom were near, he would help me find it. Twenty minutes after I finished writing, I found the locket. Coincidence or help from above?

The other thing that happened was interesting. We were at my other son's house, sitting in the living room. My son David, his wife Cathy, my daughter Nanci and her husband Brent, my husband, and our little grandson were together. There was a loud knock at the front door. We all heard it. My son's house was in a new, incomplete development. Few houses and trees. My son opened the door. He looked up and down the street. No people, no cars. We decided it was Tom letting us know he was there.

Many of my communications seem to start with a phone ring. On August 20, 1993, I again heard a phone ring. I did not pick up the phone by my bed, but instead I asked who was in the room. I was not afraid and was told, "It is I." That was all he said. Here is where my English grammar failed me. I would say, "It's me." Apparently, this is incorrect grammar. The voice was that of a man. I had never heard that voice before. It was the most beautiful voice I have ever heard. It was soft yet strong and oh-so gentle. Several weeks later while in my Bible study class, we were discussing one of the Gospels. There it was in print. Jesus was quoted, saying, "It is I." Then it all clicked. Jesus was the presence in my bedroom. What a marvelous blessing. I am certain Jesus was letting me know he knows all of his children, and he was aware of my suffering. Had I read the Bible verse first, I would have considered it a figment of my imagination.

When my husband and I were visiting our son, David, and Cathy; they relayed the following event: Both of them worked away from home. When they came home from work, they checked their answering machine because the light was blinking. When they turned on the machine, there was only one message, and it was from Tom. It was not a new message. It was an old one they apparently never erased. It was about Tom having left some keys at their house when he had visited them. I believe it was Tom letting them know that his spirit was around.

Apparently prayers do not have to be prayed aloud to be heard. I silently prayed that my precious son would make himself known to me. I was in bed, not really asleep but not fully awake. I was on my left side. I felt a warmth enveloping my body. It was not the usual tingle. It started from my back and felt warm, loving, and gentle. The words sincere and kind also came to mind. My first thought was that my husband had covered me. When I became fully conscious, I looked at my husband. He was on the other side of the bed snoring. Since it wasn't my husband and no one else was in the house, I can only think that it was a heavenly body. Whatever or whoever it was, I do not know. It never spoke to me. I would like to think it was Tom, but I really don't know.

There are dreams and then there are other dreams. I cannot watch horror films or murder mysteries on TV. I have horrible dreams afterward. The dreams I believe in are those that catch me by total surprise, meaning there was no event during my waking hours related to anything about which I was dreaming. Nor was I thinking about them as I went to sleep. Some of my dreams occur around 1:00 a.m. Most, however, are between 5:00 a.m. and 6:00 a.m. I have had visions of things just before I awaken. These are brief glimpses usually of things, but I am not sure how they relate to my future. What I do believe is that one's body must be at total rest and relaxation for anything spiritual to happen. That is why I couldn't reach Tom shortly after his death on this plane.

I did have a strange dream about three years after Tom died. I was floating over a very clear lake. I saw several objects in the water. Apparently, I was showing these things to a man I did not know. He was thin and had dark hair and eyes. I told him my son's dresser was under the water. He said he knew that, and the dresser had steel pins in it that I know nothing about. He also said he hoped the dresser would last longer than my son. I asked him if he knew my son's name. He replied, "Tom." At this point, we had moved away from the lake, and I was following him down a hallway. I do recall asking the man his name, but he did not reply. One thing he did say was that Tom was still growing up. I thought that was a stupid thing to say. Tom died at twenty-two, was very smart, and had wisdom far above his years. However, I also do recall seeing Tom as a baby, then two years old, and later at four years old, and again later at eight to ten years old.

A stern-looking older woman (like a not-so-nice grandma) was standing in the hallway. She seemed angry that I was there. I got the impression she was there to stop me from entering the room. I walked through her and awakened. It was 6:35 a.m.

In March of 1994, I had an experience I will never forget. My husband had told me that he had a dream where he hugged our son. Since Tom died instantly in the car crash, I never had the opportunity to say goodbye to him. In prayer, I asked God and my angels for the opportunity to hug him again and say goodbye. For whatever reason, it didn't occur to me to say my goodbyes when I first saw him in the mansion.

In my dream, a group of people took me to an empty room. I didn't know the people, but they seemed nice and were smiling. The room had four walls and a doorway. I was not aware of a ceiling or a floor. As I was standing there, Tom walked through the doorway. I held out my arms, and he walked over to me. His hug was firm, and I felt his body. This was not a spirit. This felt like a real body. It was a long hug and so tight. Naturally I hugged him back. We never talked. When I awoke, I thanked God and my angels for allowing this to happen. God does answer prayers. The hug was my way of saying goodbye. Many years have passed since that event, but it remains as clear in my mind as the day it happened.

The day before my experience, I was watching TV, and a man was talking about "mystical experiences." He talked about an "electrical feeling." I wish I had gotten his name. He confirmed what I have felt numerous times. Now I know I am not alone, and above all that, I am not nuts. I know there is life after earthly death, and one day I will be with Tom again. Maybe then I will be able to learn what really caused the accident.

As the months and years progressed, the pain of losing Tom was not as raw. I was adjusting to my loss. That doesn't mean I didn't occasionally cry or that I stopped missing him. There will always be a hole in my heart, and my love for him will never end.

So many times since Tom died I had asked to be able to communicate with Tom more often. Then in January of 1996, I had what started out as a weird dream. There were two children with me. We were in a long building. The front part appeared to be a hospital. For whatever reason, I had just set my hair and decided to go to what I knew was my apartment at the rear of this long building. I was then alone. I have no idea what happened to the children.

When I entered the apartment, I noticed that the door was unlocked, the lights were on, and I thought there was a dog on the bed. I felt someone was there, but I was not afraid. I opened my closet door. The light was on in the closet, but there were no clothes. Then I opened another door. Again, the light was on. I said, "Tom?" With that, I saw him standing in front of me. This time, we had a conversation. Tom was tall but thinner than I remembered. He wore a white shirt and greenish slacks. That was the color of his Armani suit. His hands were stretched out to me. I asked him if I could touch him. He replied, "Yes." At first I touched his hands. Then I hugged him and told him how much I loved him. He told me he loved me too.

I asked him if the accident was really an accident or if it was supposed to happen. He said again it was an accident. (The various mediums and psychics I have questioned about this told me his death was preordained and planned by Tom before he incarnated. Which explanation is correct? I cannot answer that. I am only going by what Tom told me.) Tom also said something about "the entrance wasn't like it used to be" but that you had to "go with the flow." He seemed resigned and adjusted. I am not sure what all that means except that we cannot mess with the laws of nature set by God. When the broken rib punctured his heart, he died.

I asked Tom if I would see him again, he indicated that it was possible. For sure, he did not say no. I awoke with a jolt at 4:37 a.m.

I thanked God and my angels for the visit. I can't explain it to nonbelievers, but

I know this was more than a dream. This really happened—I did speak with him, he answered me, and I did hug him.

The years have slipped by. I talk to Tom but don't really get answers. I have had to release him so he can do his job in heaven. His life is there, and mine is here. I did have a dream several years ago where Tom, his buddy who died in the accident, and I were in a lake. I saw them walk away from me. They went one way, and I walked in another direction. That told me I needed to let them go their way. It was not yet time for me to be with him.

My husband died in 2010. At this writing, I have been a widow for thirteen years. About seven years ago, a man I have known since high school came into my life. After two years of dating, we decided to live together. His young grandson was living outside Chicago, and he wanted to see him grow up. I pulled up roots, and we moved to the

Chicago area. Our home was in a new golfing development. At the edge of our property was a bridge over a pond with the golf course at the far side of the bridge. In the middle of the bridge, there is a gazebo. That became my special place to talk to Tom on a daily basis. All the conversations were one way, but I felt at peace there.

Then one night while sleeping, I saw Tom. He seemed so sad. It really bothered me. I thought heaven was supposed to be a happy place. It hurt me that he wasn't happy. I wrote to a friend I had consulted in recent years who is a spiritual counselor and intuitive reader. She is able to communicate with the angel Michael. I explained my concern about Tom being so sad. She looked into it and came back with an explanation.

Tom's job in heaven is to help lost souls find their way back to the light. He does not look for them, but they find each other. I consider the light to be God. He was having a problem with an infant soul. She asked me if I had ever had an abortion or if my mother had. The answer was no, but my mother had miscarried a boy when I was three years old. The story my mother told me was that when she was three months pregnant, the neighbors told her she *had* to give me a birthday party. That meant walking into town, shopping for ice cream, cake, etc., and giving me a party. I was three years old at the time and remember nothing. That night my mother had a miscarriage. Apparently, the soul of this infant was wandering and never made it back to heaven. Tom knew I would get help for him. Thanks to the intervention of archangel Michael, the problem was solved, and the infant's soul was returned to heaven.

Shortly after all this happened, Tom appeared to me again in a dream. This time, I decided to hug him as I had done before. However, the outcome was very different. Over the years, he had become ethereal. When I hugged him, I went right through him. I was hugging air. Over the many years of reading about the afterlife, I learned our bodies gradually get lighter and become ethereal. Think of the cartoons of *Casper*, the friendly ghost. He can go through things. Casper isn't real but the concept is.

Something else happened to me totally unrelated to Tom. It happened somewhere around 2012. I had gone to Spring Hill, Florida, for the winter. I needed surgery that my local hospital was unable to do. I decided to have the surgery at Tampa General. I was also dealing with some personal problems. I had gone to bed. My dear dog, Biscuit, was on the bed with me. For whatever reason I opened my eyes and looked toward the ceiling. There floating above me was a man dressed in what seemed like a white toga with a gold braid around his waist and crossed across his chest. Everything went very fast. The man had a ruddy complexion, gray curly hair, and he was smiling. I was scared beyond belief. I screamed, and Biscuit gave me a funny look. Apparently he was not seeing what I was seeing. The man never spoke to me, maybe because I told him to leave and never come back. With that, he swooshed across the ceiling into the closet and out from there.

I have never seen him again. Now I wish I had been a little composed. Maybe he was going to give an important message. Now I wish he would return. Was he my guide? Maybe, but I probably will never know if he doesn't return.

I have not seen Tom recently. I love him more than life but accept that he has his own life where he is, and I must live my life on earth until I am called home. Without loving him any less, I have let go so he can do the job given to him by our Heavenly Father.

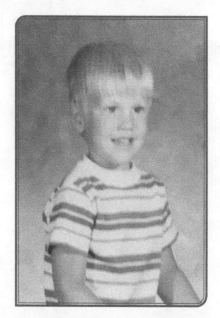

ABOUT THE AUTHOR

A n i t a Hargreaves is a loving mother and grand-  mother. Her husband died one day short of their forty-ninth anni- versary. After living in several states and also living in Pakistan as a teenager, she now calls the mountains of North Car- olina home. There she enjoys the beauty of nature and the peace that comes with that beauty. She is a graduate of Cen- tenary University and, as a senior cit- izen, received an AA degree in floral design from Erwin Technical School in Tampa, Florida. She enjoys cooking, especially on rainy days. Her surviving children and grandchildren are her special delight.